The Art of Cooking Pumpkin

Pumpkin

Over 25 Delicious Pumpkin Recipes and
Pumpkin Pie Recipes You Will Love

By

Ted Alling

License Notes

No part of this Book can be reproduced in any form or by any means including print, electronic, scanning or photocopying unless prior permission is granted by the author.

All ideas, suggestions and guidelines mentioned here are written for informative purposes. While the author has taken every possible step to ensure accuracy, all readers are advised to follow information at their own risk. The author cannot be held responsible for personal and/or commercial damages in case of misinterpreting and misunderstanding any part of this Book

Table of Contents

Introduction

It is that time of year where it seems that pumpkin is taking over the planet. You will find pumpkin in nearly everything being sold in stores today such as pumpkin lattes, pumpkin iced coffees, pumpkin scones, pumpkin bread and even pumpkin cookies. You name it, there is pumpkin in it.

During the fall season pumpkin seems to be synonymous with the holiday season so it is no wonder why people get excited for it. If you are a huge fan of pumpkin recipes, then this is the perfect book for you. Inside of this cookbook you are going to discover the wonders of cooking with pumpkin. You will also find a variety of delicious pumpkin recipes you won't be able to get enough of such as pumpkin packed waffles, pumpkin stews and pumpkin muffins.

So, let's not waste any more time. Let's get cooking!

Savory Pumpkin Recipes

Pumpkin Packed Black Been and Beef Chili

Pumpkin chili itself is incredibly delicious, but with the help of this recipe you can enjoy an incredibly savory dish that I know you are going to fall in love with. It is a great chili recipe to make during the fall season to get you into the festive mood.

Makes: 6 Servings

Total Prep Time: 1 Hour and 5 Minutes

Ingredients for Your Chili:

- 1 ¼ Pound of Round, Ground Variety

- 1 Onion, Sweet Variety and Finely Diced

- 1 Red Bell Pepper, Fresh and Finely Diced

- 3 Cloves of Garlic, Minced

- 2 Tbsp. of Chili, Powdered Variety

- 1 Tbsp. of Oregano, Dried

- 1 ½ tsp. of Cumin, Ground Variety

- 3 Cups of Pumpkin, Sweet Variety

- 1, 4 Ounce Can of Black Beans

- 1, 8 Ounce Can of Tomatoes, Fire Roasted Variety and Finely Diced

- 1, 16 Ounce Can of Beef Broth, Homemade Preferable

- 1 ¼ tsp. of Salt, For Taste

- 1 tsp. of Black Pepper, For Taste

- 1/3 Cup of Cilantro, Fresh and Roughly Chopped

- Some Jalapenos, Thinly Sliced

- Some Sour Cream, Chipotle Style and Recipe Below

Ingredients for Your Chipotle Sour Cream:

- 1, 8 Ounce Container of Sour Cream, Soft

- 1 tsp. of Chipotle Chiles in Adobo Sauce, Minced and Canned

- 2 tsp. of Lime Zest, Fresh

- 1 Tbsp. of Lime Juice, Fresh

Directions:

1. The first thing that you will want to do is place your beef into a large sized Dutch oven placed over medium or high heat. Cook for at least 8 minutes or until your beef is fully brown in color. Remove and transfer to a container.

2. Add your diced onions to your Dutch oven and cook in your beef drippings for the next 7 minutes. Add in your powdered chili, dried oregano and ground cumin. Stir to combine and continue to cook for another minutes.

3. Add in your pumpkin, black beans, finely diced tomatoes and homemade beef broth. Season with a dash of salt and pepper and stir to combine.

4. Bring this mixture to a boil before reducing the heat to low. Allow your mixture to simmer for the next 20 to 25 minutes or until your pumpkin is tender to the touch. Add in your fresh cilantro and season again with a dash of salt and pepper. Remove from heat.

5. Next make your chipotle sour cream. To do this use a small sized bowl and add in all of your ingredients for your sour cream. Stir thoroughly to combine and season with a dash of salt and pepper.

6. Serve your chili with a dollop of your sour cream over the top and enjoy while still piping hot.

Pumpkin Style Cannelloni Smothered in Sage and Brown Butter Sauce

If you love the taste of traditional cannelloni, then this is one dish I know you are going to fall in love with. It is a creative twist on a classic cannelloni dish that is packed full of pumpkin, giving it a unique and delicious taste you will want to enjoy over and over again.

Makes: 6 Servings

Total Prep Time: 1 Hour and 20 Minutes

Ingredients:

- 1 ½ Pound of Pumpkin, Fresh

- 1 ½ Tbsp. of Olive oil, Extra Virgin Variety

- 3 Cloves of Garlic, Minced

- ½ Cup of Ricotta, Soft

- ½ Cup of Parmigiano-Reggiano Cheese, Freshly Grated

- 1 ½ tsp. of Sage, Fresh and Roughly Chopped

- ¼ tsp. of Salt, For Taste

- ½ tsp. of Black Pepper, For Taste

- 1 Pack of Lasagna Sheets, Oven Ready Variety

- 6 Tbsp. of Butter, Unsalted Variety and Soft

Directions:

1. The first thing that you will want to do is preheat your oven to 350 degrees.

2. While your oven is heating up place your pumpkin along with at least ¾ cup of water into a large sized skillet placed over medium heat. Cover your skillet and steam your pumpkin for the next 20 minutes or until tender to the touch. After this time remove your pumpkin and mash thoroughly in a large sized bowl until smooth in consistency.

3. Next heat up some olive oil in a small sized skillet placed over medium heat. Add in your garlic and cook until gold in color. Once golden transfer your garlic into a mortar and pestle. Crush thoroughly until a paste begins to form.

4. Then add in your ricotta and parmigiana Reggiano cheese. Add in your sage, dash of salt and pepper and stir to combine. Then transfer to your mashed pumpkin mixture and set aside for later use.

5. Next bring a large sized pot of water to a boil. Once your water is boiling add in your lasagna sheets and cook for the next 2 minutes or until tender to the touch. Once cooked transfer to a place and drizzle a bit of olive oil over the top. Make sure that you reserve at least ¼ cup of your pasta water.

6. Brush a large sized baking dish with a generous amount of oil. Then place on tender sheet of lasagna onto a flat surface. Add at least 4 spoonfuls of your pumpkin mixture into the center and roll to form a cannelloni tube. Transfer to your prepared baking dish and repeat until your pumpkin mixture has been used.

7. Pour your reserved pasta water over your lasagna and cover your dish with some aluminum foil.

8. Place into your oven to bake for the next 20 to 25 minutes or until your pasta is completely heated through.

9. While your pasta is cook add your butter and fresh sage leaves into a small sized skillet and place over medium to high heat. Cook for the next 5 minutes or until your butter mixture is at least golden brown in color. Remove from heat and drizzle this over your pasta dish.

10. Allow to cool slightly before serving.

Harvest Style Pumpkin Soup

If you are looking for a hearty soup recipe to serve up whenever you need a bit of warming up or filling, then this is the perfect soup dish for you to make. For the lightest and healthiest results, feel free to substitute your chicken broth with some heavy cream instead.

Makes: 8 Servings

Total Prep Time: 1 Hour

Ingredients:

- 2 Tbsp. of Butter, Unsalted Variety and Soft

- 1 Potato, Large in Size and Finely Diced

- 4 ½ Cups of Chicken Broth, Homemade Preferable

- 1, 8 Ounce Can of Pumpkin, Pure

- Dash of Salt and Black Pepper, For Taste

- ¼ tsp. of Nutmeg, Ground Variety

- ½ Pint of Heavy Cream

Directions:

1. Use a large sized pot and place over medium heat. Add in your butter and once your butter is fully melted add in your onions and potato. Cook for the next 8 minutes or until your onions are translucent.

2. Then add in your homemade chicken broth. Bring your mixture to a boil. Once boiling reduce the heat to low and then continue to cook for the next 10 to 12 minutes or until your potatoes are tender to the touch.

3. Add in your pumpkin and stir thoroughly to combine.

4. Transfer your soup to a blender. Blend on the highest setting or until smooth in consistency. Pour back into your pot and set over low heat.

5. Season your soup with a dash of salt and pepper and ground nutmeg.

6. Increase the heat to medium or high and bring to a boil. Once boiling reduce the heat to low and continue to cook for the next 10 minutes.

7. Add in your cream and season with a dash of salt and pepper. Stir to combine and remove from heat. Serve while still piping hot.

Risotto Packed with Pumpkin

This pumpkin risotto is perfect if you are a huge fan of risotto. Packed full of a delicious and nutritious flavor, I know this is one dish you won't be able to get enough of. Thick and creamy, this is one dish you will want to enjoy over and over again.

Makes: 8 Servings

Total Prep Time: 1 Hour and 25 Minutes

Ingredients:

- 2 Tbsp. of Olive oil, Extra Virgin Variety

- 1 Tbsp. of Onion, Finely Diced

- 2 Cups of Pumpkin, Fresh

- 2 Cups of Rice, Arborio Variety

- 2 to 3 Tbsp. of White Wine, Dry Variety

- 6 Cups of Chicken Broth, Homemade Preferable

- 1 Sprig of Rosemary, Fresh Variety

- 4 to 5 Mushrooms, Porcini Variety and Dried

- 2 Tbsp. of Butter, Unsalted Variety and Soft

- ¾ Cup of Parmesan Cheese, Finely Grated

- Dash of Salt and Pepper, For Taste

Directions:

1. Use a large sized saucepan and place over medium to high heat. Add in your oil and once your oil is hot enough add in your onions. Cook until soft to the touch. This should take at least 5 minutes.

2. After this time add in your pumpkin and continue to cook for another 6 to 8 minutes, making sure to stir your mixture often.

3. Then add in your rice and stir thoroughly until fully coated in your oil. Then add in your wine and stir thoroughly to combine.

4. Next add in your homemade broth, fresh rosemary and mushrooms. Stir to combine and bring this mixture to a boil. Once boiling reduce the heat to low and bring it to a simmer. Simmer until most of your liquid has been absorbed and your rice is tender to the touch. This should take at least 18 minutes.

5. After this time add in your butter and at least ¼ cup of your Parmesan cheese. Stir thoroughly to combine.

6. Remove from heat and season with a dash of salt and pepper and top off with your remaining Parmesan cheese before serving.

Pumpkin and Ricotta Stuffed Shells

If you are a huge fan of traditional Italian style stuffed shells, then this is one dish I know you are going to love. Packed full of a tasty pumpkin taste, I know this is one dish you won't be able to get enough of.

Makes: 8 Servings

Total Prep Time: 1 Hour and 35 Minutes

Ingredients:

- 24 Pasta Shells, Jumbo Variety

- 1 Tbsp. of Olive Oil, Extra Virgin Variety

- 22 Ounces of Ricotta Cheese, Fat Free Variety

- 1, 8 Ounce Can of Pumpkin, Fresh

- 2 ½ Ounces of Pecorino Romano Cheese, Freshly Grated

- 1 Egg, Large in Size and White Only

- 2 Cloves of Garlic, Minced

- 1 Cup of Basil, Fresh and Roughly Chopped

- 1 Tbsp. of Sage, Fresh and Roughly Chopped

- 1 tsp. of Salt, For Taste

- 1 tsp. of Black Pepper, For Taste

- 1, 8 Ounce Jar of Tomato Sauce, Your Favorite Kind

Directions:

1. First cook your pasta shells according to the directions on the package. Once fully cooked drain your pasta and place onto a baking sheet. Drizzle with a bit of oil and set aside for later use.

2. Next use a medium sized bowl and add in your ricotta cheese, pumpkin, at least ¾ cup of your Romano, large egg, minced garlic, fresh basil, fresh sage and dash of salt and pepper. Stir to thoroughly combine.

3. Then preheat your oven to 350 degrees.

4. While your oven is heating up spread your tomato sauce into the bottom of a large sized baking dish.

5. Next fill each of your cooked shells with at least three spoonfuls of your pumpkin and ricotta cheese mixture. Place into your baking dish. Cover with some aluminum foil and place into your oven to bake for the next 30 minutes.

6. After this time remove your aluminum foil and top off with your remaining cheese. Place back into your oven to back for an additional 15 minutes.

7. Remove from your oven and allow to cool slightly before serving.

Ginger and Pumpkin Waffles

Love the taste of waffles? Then you are going to fall in love with this dish. You can serve these waffles up during the fall season when you want to give yourself a delicious breakfast meal to enjoy.

Makes: 5 Servings

Total Prep Time: 30 Minutes

Ingredients:

- 1 ¼ Cup of Flour, All Purpose Variety

- 1 ½ tsp. of Baker's Style Baking Powder

- ½ tsp. of Baker's Style Baking Soda

- ¼ tsp. of Salt, For Taste

- 2 tsp. of Ginger, Ground Variety

- ½ tsp. of Cinnamon, Ground

- ¼ Cup of Ginger, Crystallized Variety and Finely Chopped

- 2 Eggs, Large in Size and Beaten

- ¾ Cup of Buttermilk, Whole

- ½ Cup of Pumpkin, Canned Variety and Pureed Variety

- ½ Cup of Sugar, White in Color

- ¾ tsp. of Vanilla, Pure

- 3 Tbsp. of Butter, Unsalted Variety and Soft

Directions:

1. Use a large sized bowl and add in your flour, baker's style baking powder, baker's style baking soda, dash of salt, ground ginger and ground cinnamon. Stir thoroughly to combine.

2. Remove at least two spoonfuls of your flour mixture and add to a medium sized bowl. Add in your ginger to your separate flour mixture. Stir thoroughly to combine.

3. Then use a medium sized bowl and add in your large eggs, whole buttermilk, white sugar, pure vanilla and pumpkin. Stir well to combine. Add in your butter and ginger mixture, making sure to fold to incorporate.

4. Next preheat a waffle iron to high heat. Once your waffle iron is hot enough add in at least ½ cup of your batter and cook until fully cooked through. Repeat until all of your batter has been used. Serve with your favorite syrup.

Curried Peas and Pumpkin

Here is another pumpkin dish that I know you won't be able to get enough of. It is seasoned with a dash of curry powder to make a dish that is packed full of spice that you won't want to put down.

Makes: 6 Servings

Total Prep Time: 45 Minutes

Ingredients:

- 2 Tbsp. of Butter, Unsalted Variety and Soft

- 1 Onion, Medium in Size and Finely Diced

- 1 Clove of Garlic, Minced

- 2 ½ tsp. of Curry, Powdered Variety

- ½ tsp. of Salt, For Taste

- ½ tsp. of Black Pepper, For Taste

- 2 Pounds of Pumpkin, Fresh

- 2 Red Potatoes, Medium in Size and Cut into Quarters

- 1 ½ Cup of Chicken Broth, Low in Sodium and Homemade Preferable

- ¾ Cup of Raisins, Golden in Color

- ¾ Cup of Peas, Baby Variety, Frozen and Thawed

- Some Cilantro, Fresh and Roughly Chopped

Directions:

1. First heat up a large sized pan placed over medium to high heat. Add in your butter and once your butter is fully melted add in your onions. Cook for the next 5 minutes or until golden brown in color.

2. Once golden brown add in your garlic and cook for an additional minute.

3. Next add in your powdered curry, dash of salt and pepper.

4. Add in your pumpkin and potatoes and continue to cook for another 5 minutes. Make sure that stir frequently as it cooks.

5. Add in your broth and raisins. Stir to combine and reduce the heat to medium. Cook for at least 15 minutes before adding in your peas.

6. Cover and continue to cook for the next 5 to 10 minutes or until your potatoes and pumpkin are tender to the touch. Remove from heat and serve with a garnish of cilantro.

Hearty Roasted Pumpkin Soup Packed with Mushrooms

Here is yet another filling pumpkin soup recipe that I know you won't be able to get enough of. It is packed full of herb flecked mushrooms and topped off with some fresh chives to make a delicious meal that can accompany your main Thanksgiving meal.

Makes: 8 Servings

Total Prep Time: 1 Hour and 55 Minutes

Ingredients for Your Soup:

- 1 Pumpkin, Fresh

- 3 Tbsp. of Olive Oil, Extra Virgin Variety

- 1 Onion, Medium in Size and Finely Diced

- 2 Leeks, Small in Size and White and Green Parts Separated

- 1 Potato, Russet Variety

- 1 Stalk of Celery, Fresh

- 2 Cloves of Garlic, Minced

- 6 Cups of Chicken Broth, Homemade Preferable

- 2 tsp. of Salt, For Taste

- ½ tsp. of Black Pepper, For Taste

Ingredients for Your Mushroom Topping:

- 1 Tbsp. of Olive oil, Extra Virgin Variety

- 1 Tbsp. of Butter, Unsalted Variety and Soft

- 3 Cups of Mushrooms, Wild Variety and Assorted

- 1 Tbsp. of Shallots, Minced

- 2 Tbsp. of Chives, Fresh and Trimmed

- 1 tsp. of Thyme Leaves, Fresh and Roughly Chopped

- ¼ tsp. of Salt, For Taste

- ¼ tsp. of Black Pepper, For Taste

Directions:

1. The first thing that you will want to do is make your soup. To do this preheat your oven to 425 degrees. While your oven is heating up use a large sized roasting pan and add in your pumpkin. Toss with a dash of olive oil until thoroughly coated. Place into your oven to roast for the next 45 minutes or until tender to the touch.

2. While your pumpkin is roasting heat up some more oil in a large sized Dutch oven placed over medium heat. Once your oil is hot enough add in your onions, potato, fresh celery, fresh leeks and minced garlic. Cook for at least 2 minutes. Making sure that you stir constantly.

3. Cover and reduce the heat to low. Cook your veggies for the next 20 minutes until tender to the touch, making sure to stir at least once.

4. Add in your roasted pumpkin and broth. Bring your mixture to a boil and reduce the heat to low. Allow to simmer for the next 30 minutes, making sure to stir frequently.

5. Transfer your mixture into a blender. Season with a dash of salt and pepper. Blend on the highest setting until smooth in consistency.

6. Next make your mushroom topping. To do this heat up your oil and butter in a large sized skillet placed over medium to high heat. Once your oil is hot enough add in your mushrooms and shallots. Cook for at least 4 minutes or until tender to the touch.

7. Remove from heat and season with a dash of salt and pepper. Add in your chives and thyme and stir to combine. Serve your soup and top off with your mushroom. Enjoy!

Filling Pumpkin Bread

Looking for a tasty bread recipe to serve up alongside your holiday meal? Then this is the perfect bread dish for you to make. It is a dish that you can enjoy any time of the day, regardless if you are serving it alongside your main dish or enjoying it as a tasty snack.

Makes: 8 Servings

Total Prep Time: 1 Hour and 20 Minutes

Ingredients:

- 2 Sticks of Butter, Unsalted Variety and Soft

- 2 ½ Cups of Flour, All Purpose Variety

- 1 Cup of Brown Sugar, Light and Packed

- 1 Cup of Sugar, Granulated Variety

- 2 tsp. of Baker's Style Baking Powder

- 1 tsp. of Baker's Style Baking Soda

- 2 tsp. of Cinnamon, Ground Variety

- ¾ tsp. of Cloves, Ground Variety

- 2 Cups of Pumpkin, Freshly Grated

- 3 Eggs, Large in Size and Beaten

- ½ Cup of Buttermilk, Whole

- 1 ½ tsp. of Vanilla, Pure

Directions:

1. The first thing that you will want to do is preheat your oven to 350 degrees. While your oven is heating up butter and flour two large sized loaf pans. Set aside for later use.

2. Next use a large sized bowl and add in your flour, brown sugar, white sugar, baker's style baking powder, baker's style baking soda, ground cinnamon and ground cloves. Stir thoroughly to combine. Add in your pumpkin into this mixture and toss thoroughly to combine.

3. Use a medium sized bowl and add in your eggs, whole buttermilk, soft butter and pure vanilla. Whisk thoroughly until evenly mixed. Add in your dry ingredients and stir to combine.

4. Transfer your mixture into both of your pans.

5. Place into your oven to bake for the next 35 minutes or until your bread is fully cooked through.

6. Remove your bread and allow to cool before removing from your pans. Slice and serve whenever you are ready.

Hearty Pumpkin Chowder

This is the perfect dish for you to serve up for your guests as your next party event. It is packed full of that delicious pumpkin flavor; I guarantee your guests will be begging you for the recipe.

Makes: 8 Servings

Total Prep Time: 1 Hour

Ingredients:

- 3 Tbsp. of Olive Oil, Extra Virgin Variety

- 2 Leeks, Fresh and Green and White Parts Separated

- 3 Cloves of Garlic, Minced

- 2 Bell Peppers, Medium in Size and Finely Diced

- 2 ¼ Pound of Pumpkin, Canned Variety

- 1 ½ tsp. of Marjoram, Fresh and Roughly Chopped

- ¼ tsp. of Red Pepper Flakes, Crushed

- 2 Bay Leaves, Fresh and Dried

- ¼ tsp. of Salt, For Taste

- ¼ tsp. of Black Pepper, For Taste

- 1 ¼ Cup of Corn, Frozen and Thawed Variety

- 6 Cups of Vegetable Broth, Homemade Preferable

Directions:

1. Heat up some oil in a large sized pot placed over medium heat. Once your oil is hot enough add in your leeks and cook for at least 5 minutes or until soft to the touch.

2. Add in your minced garlic and continue to cook for the next 2 minutes.

3. After this time add in your green peppers and reduce the heat to low or medium. Cook for the next 8 minutes or until your peppers are soft to the touch.

4. Add in your remaining ingredients and continue to cook until your pumpkin is tender to the touch. This should take at least 30 minutes.

5. Transfer your mixture into a blender. Blend on the highest setting until smooth in consistency. Transfer back into your pot and cook until piping hot.

6. Remove from heat and serve.

Cauliflower and Pumpkin Casserole

This is one pumpkin dish that you will want to serve up if you are looking for a healthy vegetable packed fish to enjoy. This dish is topping off with hearty pumpkin seeds and bread crumbs that you are going to want to enjoy over and over again.

Makes: 8 Servings

Total Prep Time: 1 Hour

Ingredients:

- 1 Cup of Bread Crumbs, Whole Wheat Variety
- ½ Cup of Pumpkin Seeds, Hulled and Roasted Variety
- 1 Tbsp. of Butter, Unsalted Variety and Soft
- 1 tsp. of Thyme Leaves, Fresh and Dried
- ¾ Cup of Goat Cheese, Crumbled
- 1 Pumpkin, Fresh
- 1 Head of Cauliflower, Fresh
- 2 Tbsp. of Flour, All Purpose Variety
- 2 Cloves of Garlic, minced
- 2 tsp. of Mustard Seeds
- 1 ½ tsp. of Salt, For Taste
- 1 tsp. of Cumin Seeds
- ½ tsp. of Black Pepper, For Taste
- 1 ½ Cups of Half and Half

Directions:

1. First assemble your vegetables. To do this first preheat your oven to 400 degrees. While your oven is heating up butter a large sized casserole dish. Set aside for later use.

2. Then use a medium sized bowl and add in your bread crumbs, pumpkin seeds, soft butter and at least half of your thyme. Stir to combine.

3. Add in your goat cheese and stir again to evenly incorporate. Slice your pumpkin and cauliflower into quarters.

4. Using a separate small sized bowl add in your flour, mustard seeds, dash of salt, ground cumin seeds, dash of pepper and remaining thyme. Stir thoroughly to combine.

5. Spread at least 1/3 of your pumpkin into the bottom of your casserole dish. Sprinkle with at least 2 spoonfuls of your flour mixture. Repeat with at least half of your cauliflower. Continue to layer into your casserole dish until all of your ingredients have been used.

6. Pour your half and half over the top and place into your oven to bake for the next 30 minutes.

7. While your casserole is baking add your remaining bread crumb mixture over your casserole after the initial 30 minutes. Return back into your oven to bake for an additional 30 minutes or until golden brown in color. Remove from your oven and serve while still hot. Enjoy.

Decadent Cream Cheese and Pumpkin Muffins

If you are looking for a simple yet delicious muffin recipe to put together, then this is the perfect dish for you to make. It is so delicious even the pickiest of eaters in your household won't be able to get enough of them.

Makes: 24 Servings

Total Prep Time: 35 Minutes

Ingredients:

- 8 Ounces of Cream Cheese, Soft

- 3 Eggs, Large in Size and Beaten Lightly

- 2 ½ Cups of Flour, All Purpose Variety

- 2 ½ Cups of Flour, All Purpose Variety

- ¼ Cup of Pecans, Finely Chopped

- 3 Tbsp. of Butter, Soft

- 2 ½ tsp. of Cinnamon, Ground Variety

- ½ tsp. of Salt, For Taste

- 2 tsp. of Baker's Style Baking Powder

- ¼ tsp. of Baker's Style Baking Soda

- 1 ¼ Cup of Pumpkin, Canned Variety and Soft

- 1/3 Cup of Oil, Vegetable Variety

- ½ tsp. of Vanilla, Pure

Directions:

1. The first thing that you will want to do is preheat your oven to 375 degrees. While your oven is heating up coat at least two muffin pans with a generous amount of oil. Set aside for later use.

2. Next use a small sized bowl and add in your soft cream cheese, large egg, and at least three tablespoons of sugar. Whisk thoroughly to combine and set aside for later use.

3. Add at least 5 tablespoons of sugar, half cup of flour, chopped pecans, soft butter and half a teaspoons of cinnamon into a medium sized bowl. Stir to combine and set aside for later use.

4. Add your remaining white sugar, flour, dash of salt, baker's style baking powder, baker's style baking soda and ground cinnamon into a large sized bowl.

5. Add your remaining eggs, soft pumpkin, oil and pure vanilla into a medium sized bowl. Make a well in the center of your flour mixture and pour in your pumpkin mixture. Stir well to thoroughly combine. Evenly divide up your batter among your muffin cups.

6. Place at least two spoonfuls of your cream cheese filling in the center of each muffin cup. Fill your muffin cups with your remaining batter.

7. Sprinkle some of your pecan mixture over the top and place into your oven to bake until golden in color and full cooked through. This should take at least 20 to 25 minutes.

8. Remove and allow to cool slightly before serving.

Pumpkin Goat Cheese Smothered Fettuccine Alfredo

If you are a huge fan of classic fettucine alfredo, then this is one dish I know you are going to absolutely love. It is relatively easy to make and can be ready on your table in just a matter of minutes, making it simple for even the most novice of cooks to make.

Makes: 2 Servings

Total Prep Time: 15 Minutes

Ingredients:

- 6 Ounces of Pasta, Gluten Free Variety

- 1 Tbsp. of Butter, Soft

- 1 Clove of Garlic, Finely Chopped

- 1 Cup of Heavy Cream

- ½ Cup of Pumpkin, Pureed Variety

- 4 Ounces of Goat Cheese, Soft

- ¼ Cup of Parmigiano Reggiano, Freshly Grated

- 1 Tbsp. of Sage, Fresh and Sliced Thinly

- ¼ tsp. of Pumpkin Pie Spice

- Dash of Salt and Black Pepper, For Taste

- 1 Tbsp. of Butter, Soft

- 1 Handful of Sage Leaves, Fresh and Dried

Directions:

1. The first thing that you will want to do is cook your pasta according to the directions on the package.

2. The melt your butter in a large sized pan placed over medium heat. Once your butter is fully melted add in your garlic and cook for at least one minute or until fragrant.

3. Add in your cream, pureed pumpkin, goat cheese, parmesan cheese, fresh sage and pumpkin pie spice. Stir thoroughly to combine and continue to cook until your cheese is fully melted.

4. Remove your mixture from heat and season with a dash of salt and pepper.

5. Next melt your butter in a large sized pan placed over medium heat. Add in your sage and cook until crispy.

6. Serve your sage over your hot pasta and enjoy right away.

Simple Pumpkin Fries

This is the perfect side dish to make to pair along with a hot dog or hamburger. They are packed full of that delicious pumpkin taste that you love.

Makes: 2 Servings

Total Prep Time: 40 Minutes

Ingredients:

- 2 Cups of Pumpkin, Soft and Canned

- 2 tsp. of Garlic, Powdered Variety

- ¼ tsp. of Cayenne Pepper

- 1 tsp. of Onion, Powdered Variety

- 1 Tbsp. of Olive Oil, Extra Virgin Variety

- Dash of Sea Salt, For Taste

Directions:

1. The first thing that you will want to do is preheat your oven to 400 degrees.

2. While your oven is heating up, peel and remove the seeds from your pumpkin. Cut your pumpkin into ½ inch sized fries.

3. Coat your fries in your garlic, cayenne pepper, powdered onion, and oil. Toss to coat on all side.

4. Place your fries onto a baking sheet lined with some parchment paper. Place into your oven to bake for the next 35 minutes, making sure to flip your fries at least halfway through.

5. After this time remove your fries and season with a dash of salt. Serve right away.

Delicious Baked Stuffed Pumpkin

Just like stuffed peppers, these baked stuffed pumpkin are perfect to make if you are looking for something more on the filling side. Packed full of Israeli style couscous, hearty sausage, healthy apples and sweet cranberries. This is one dish I know you are going to love.

Makes: 4 Servings

Total Prep Time: 50 Minutes

Ingredients:

- 4 Ounces of Sausage, Italian Variety and Sweet
- ½ Cup of Onions, Finely Chopped
- 1 Pumpkin, Fresh
- ½ Cup of Apples, Granny Smith Variety and Finely Chopped
- ¼ Cup of White Wine, Your Favorite Kind
- 1 Cup of Couscous, Israeli Variety
- ¼ Cup of Cranberries, Fresh and Dried
- 1 Tbsp. of Olive Oil, Extra Virgin Variety
- 1 tsp. of Thyme, Fresh and Dried
- 1 tsp. of Oregano, Fresh
- ¼ tsp. of Black Pepper, For Taste
- 4 Pumpkins, Small in Size

Directions:

1. The first thing that you will want to do is make your stuffing. To do this first preheat your oven to 350 degrees.

2. While your oven is heating up crumble up your sausage meat and place into a large sized saucepan placed over low to medium heat. Cook your sausage until brown in color. This should take at least 8 minutes.

3. After this time remove your sausage from your saucepan and increase the heat to medium. Add in your onions and at least two cups of your pumpkin. Cook for the next 5 to 7 minutes or until soft to the touch.

4. Add in your apple and cooked sausage. Continue to cook for the next 3 minutes.

5. Add in your wine and cook for another 2 minutes before removing from heat.

6. Use a large sized saucepan and add in your couscous, cranberries, oil, fresh thyme, fresh oregano, dash of salt and dash of pepper. Stir thoroughly to combine. Add in your meat mixture and toss thoroughly to combine.

7. Next bake your pumpkin. Fill up your pumpkin with your stuffing mixture and place into a large sized baking dish. Cover with some aluminum foil and place into your oven to bake for the next 25 minutes. After this time remove your aluminum foil. Continue to bake for an additional 10 minutes.

8. Remove from your oven and serve immediately.

Savory Pumpkin Pizza

If you are a huge fan of pizza, then this is one dish I know you are going to want to make. Packed full of pumpkin and smothered in cheese, this is one pizza dish that you will want to make over and over again.

Makes: 6 Servings

Total Prep Time: 40 Minutes

Ingredients:

- 1 Pizza Dough, Ready to Bake Variety

- 1 ½ Cups of Pumpkin, Pureed Variety

- 1 Onion, Sweet Variety and Finely Diced

- 1 tsp. of Sugar, White in Color

- 2 Cloves of Garlic, Minced

- 1 Shallot, Finely Diced

- ½ Tbsp. of Thyme, Fresh and Roughly Chopped

- Dash of Salt and Pepper, For Taste

- ½ Cup of Parmesan Cheese, Freshly Grated

- 2 Cups of Havarti Cheese, Freshly Grated

- 1 Cup of Arugula, Fresh

- Some Olive Oil, Extra Virgin Variety

Directions:

1. The first thing that you will want to do is preheat your oven to 350 degrees.

2. While your oven is heating up add a large sized skillet to medium heat. Add in your oil and once your oil is hot enough add in your onions and cook until slightly caramelized. This should take at least 15 to 20 minutes.

3. Add in your pumpkin, minced garlic, shallots, fresh thyme and half of your caramelized onions into a large sized bowl. Add in your parmesan cheese and season with a dash of salt and pepper.

4. Next prepare your pizza dough according to the directions on the package and place onto a pizza pan. Top off with your pumpkin mixture and sprinkle your fresh arugula and caramelized onions on the top. Top off with your Havarti cheese and season with some more salt and pepper.

5. Place into your oven to bake for the next 20 to 25 minutes or until your dough has been fully cooked through.

6. Remove after this time and allow to cool slightly before serving. Enjoy.

Vegetarian Style Pumpkin and Kale Pasta

This is the perfect dish to make if you want to impress your vegetarian friends and family. Still packed full of pumpkin yet healthy to enjoy, this is one dish that you don't have to feel guilty about enjoying.

Makes: 8 to 10 Servings

Total Prep Time: 30 Minutes

Ingredients:

- 1, 16 Ounce Pack of Rigatoni

- 1 Tbsp. of Olive Oil, Extra Virgin Variety

- 1 Onion, Medium in Size and Finely Diced

- 4 Cloves of Garlic, Minced

- 8 Ounces of Mushrooms, Cremini Variety and
  Finely Chopped

- 1 Bunch of Kale, Fresh and Chopped Roughly

- ½ Cup of White Wine, Dry Variety

- ½ to ¾ Cup of Basil, Fresh and Roughly Chopped

- 1, 15 Ounce Can of Pumpkin, Pureed Variety

- 1 Egg, Large in Size and Beaten Lightly

- 1, 15 Ounce Container of Ricotta Cheese, Part Skim
  Variety

- 2 Cups of Mozzarella Cheese, Finely Shredded

- 2 Cups of Tomato Sauce

Directions:

1. The first thing that you will want to do is preheat your oven to 350 degrees.

2. While your oven is heating up bring some water to a boil in a large sized pot. Once your water is boiling add in your pasta and cook until tender to the touch. Once tender drain and set aside for later use.

3. Heat up some oil in a large sized skillet placed over medium to high heat. Once your oil is hot enough add in your onion and cook until tender to the touch. This should take at least 5 to 7 minutes.

4. Add in your garlic after this time and continue to cook for an additional two minutes. Then add in your kale and mushrooms and continue to cook for the next 5 to 7 minutes.

5. Pour your wine into this mixture and continue to cook until your wine has been slightly reduced. Add in your fresh basil and garlic. Season with a dash of salt and pepper and turn off the heat of your stove.

6. Add your pumpkin, large egg, cheese, mozzarella cheese, your tomato sauce, fresh kale mixture and cooked pasta into a large sized bowl. Stir thoroughly to combine and season with a dash of salt and pepper.

7. Spray a large sized baking dish with some cooking spray. Pour in your mixture to this dish. Top off with your remaining mozzarella cheese.

8. Cover with some aluminum foil and place into your oven to bake for the next 25 to 30 minutes. After this time remove your aluminum foil and continue to bake for another 5 minutes or until your cheese is fully melted.

9. Remove from your oven and allow to cool slightly before serving.

Chipotle Spiced Pumpkin Veggie Burgers

Here is another vegetarian friendly dish that you can enjoy when you are looking for something more on the filling side. It is easy to make and is sure to please everyone in your household.

Makes: 4 Servings

Total Prep Time: 20 Minutes

Ingredients:

- 1 Tbsp. of Flaxseed, Ground Variety

- 3 Tbsp. of Water, Warm

- 1 Cup of Beans, Cannellini Variety

- 1 cup of Pumpkin, Puree Variety

- ½ Tbsp. of Chipotle Peppers in Adobo Sauce, Finely Chopped

- 1 Clove of Garlic, Minced

- ½ Cup of Green Onions, Finely Chopped

- ½ tsp. of Garlic, Powdered Variety

- ½ tsp. of Italian Seasoning, Salt Free Variety

- ½ tsp. of Paprika

- ¼ tsp. of Salt, For Taste

- ¼ tsp. of Red Pepper Flakes, Crushed

- 1 Tbsp. of Olive Oil, Extra Virgin Variety

- 1 ½ Cups of Oats, Rolled Variety

- 1 to 2 Cups of Salad Green, Fresh and Your Favorite Kind

- 4 Buns, Toasted and Optional

Ingredients for Your Avocado Smash:

- 1 Avocado, Fresh and Ripe

- 1/8 tsp. of Paprika

- Dash of Salt, For Taste

- Ingredients for Your Chipotle Aioli:

- 1/3 Cup of Mayonnaise, Your Favorite Kind

- 1 tsp. of Lemon Juice, Fresh

- 1 tsp. of Chipotle Adobo Sauce

- ¼ tsp. of Seasoning, Cajun Variety

- 1/8 tsp. of Cayenne Pepper, For Taste

- Dash of Salt, For Taste

Directions:

1. First make your flax egg. To do this add your ground flax and at least three spoonfuls of your water into a medium sized bowl. Stir thoroughly to combine and place into your fridge to chill until completely set.

2. Next mash up your beans in a large sized bowl and set aside for later.

3. Add your pumpkin, chipotle peppers and minced garlic to your beans. Season with a dash of salt, powdered garlic, Italian seasoning, dash of paprika, crushed red pepper flakes and green onions. Stir thoroughly to coat.

4. Place your oats into a blender and blend on the highest setting until pureed finely. Add a spoonful of oil to your oats and stir thoroughly to coat. Pour into a large sized bowl. Add in your flax egg mixture and stir again to combine. Roll your mixture into even sized balls. Firm into a hamburger shape.

5. Cover with some plastic wrap and chill in your fridge for at least 30 minutes.

6. After this time add some oil into a large sized skillet placed over medium to high heat. Once your skillet is hot enough add in your patties and cook for at least 8 to 10 minutes or until golden brown in color. Remove and serve on buns topped off with your avocado smash and your aioli sauce.

7. To make your avocado smash, mix all of your ingredients for your smash into a medium sized bowl until smooth in consistency.

8. To make your aioli add all of your ingredients for your aioli into a medium sized bowl and stir until smooth in consistency.

Delicious Pumpkin Packed Ravioli Smothered in Brown Butter Parmesan

Here is yet another Italian style dish that I know you are going to love. Smothered in a taste Sage brown butter parmesan sauce and chopped pecans, it is the perfect dish to make to satisfy those hungry eaters in your household.

Makes: 2 to 3 Servings

Total Prep Time: 35 Minutes

Ingredients:

- Dash of Salt, For Taste

- 2 Tbsp. of Olive Oil, Extra Virgin Variety

- 1 Cup of Pumpkin, Canned Variety

- 1/3 Cup of Parmesan Cheese, Freshly Grated

- Dash of Cayenne Pepper, For Taste and Optional

- Dash of Black Pepper, For Taste

- 24 Wonton Skin

- 1 Egg, Large in Size and Beaten Lightly

- 1 Stick of Butter, Unsalted Variety

- 6 Sage Leaves, Sliced Thinly

- ¼ Cup of Pecans, Lightly Toasted

Directions:

1. First bring a large sized pot filled with water to a boil. Add in a touch of oil.

2. Next use a small sized bowl and add in your canned pumpkin along with your parmesan cheese, cayenne pepper and dash of salt and pepper. Stir thoroughly to combine.

3. Place your wonton skins onto a flat surface and add in your filling evenly into the center of your skins.

4. Brush the outside of your skins with some beaten eggs and fold over to form pockets.

5. Place some butter into a large sized saucepan placed over medium heat. Once your oil is hot enough add in your butter and once your butter is hot enough reduce the heat to low and add in your sage leaves. Cook for at least 1 to 2 minutes. Remove from heat and place onto a plate lined with paper towels.

6. Drop your ravioli into your boiling water and cook for at least 2 minutes or until they begin to float to the top. Remove and drain.

7. Serve with a drizzling of your brown butter and sage over the top. Enjoy.

Healthy Roasted Pumpkin and Peach Salad

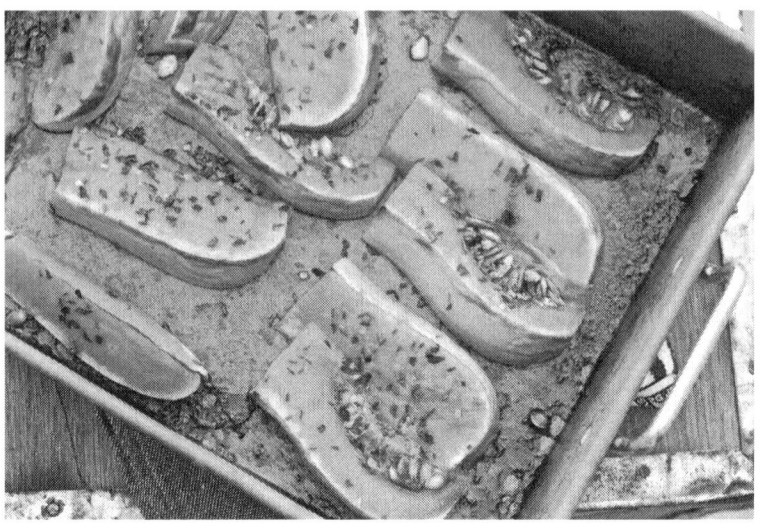

If you are looking for a healthy and nutritious salad recipe to enjoy, then this is the perfect dish for you. For the tastiest results serve this salad dish with your favorite dressing.

Makes: 1 Serving

Total Prep Time: 1 Hour

Ingredients for Your Dressing:

- 1 Pumpkin, Japanese Style, Skin and Seeds Reserved

- 6 Tbsp. of Olive Oil, Extra Virgin Variety

- 4 Tbsp. of Honey, Raw

- 2 Limes, Fresh and Juice Only

- Dash of Sea Salt and Black Pepper, For Taste

Ingredients for Your Salad:

- 2 Handfuls of Almonds, Finely Chopped

- 4 Peaches, Stone Remove and Cut into Thin Wedges

- 2 Fennels, Thinly Sliced

- 1 Head of Lettuce, Leaves Torn into Small Sized Pieces

Directions:

1. The first thing that you will want to do is preheat your oven to 430 degrees.

2. While your oven is heating up cut your pumpkin into large sized squares. Place into a large sized baking tray with the skin side facing down. Drizzle with your oil and season with a dash of sea salt. Place into your oven to bake for the next 30 to 45 minutes or until soft to the touch.

3. While your pumpkin is roasting add your oil, raw honey and fresh lime juice into a large sized bowl. Season with a dash of salt and pepper and stir to thoroughly combine.

4. Place your roasted pumpkin into a large sized bowl and pour in half of your dressing. Toss gently to coat.

5. Next add in your almond into a large sized baking tray and place into your oven to bake for the next 10 minutes or until gold in color.

6. Then place all of your ingredients for your salad into a large sized bowl. Pour in half of your dressing and toss to coat. Serve with a topping of your roasted pumpkin and garnish with your almonds. Serve right away and enjoy.

Thai Style Pumpkin Laksa with Crunchy Chickpeas

If you are a huge fan of traditional Thai food, then this is one dish I know you are going to fall in love with. Made with tasty fried chickpeas, it is the ultimate lunch or dinner recipe to prepare.

Makes: 4 Servings

Total Prep Time: 1 Hour

Ingredients:

- 1 Tbsp. of Oil, Sesame Variety

- 2 Cloves of Garlic, Minced

- 1 Inch Piece of Ginger, Freshly Grated
- 1 Red Pepper, Fresno Variety, Seeds Removed and Finely Chopped
- 2 Green Onions, Finely Chopped
- 3 ½ Cups of Chicken Broth, Homemade Preferable
- 1 Pumpkin, Small in Size, Peeled and Cut into Small Sized Cubes
- 1 Tbsp. of Peanut Butter, Creamy Variety
- 2 Tbsp. of Soy Sauce, Your Favorite Kind
- 1 Tbsp. of Fish Sauce, Homemade Preferable
- 1, 13 Ounce Can of Milk, Coconut Variety and Unsweetened
- 1 Bunch of Broccolini, Trimmed and Fresh
- ½ Cup of Cilantro, Fresh and Roughly Chopped
- ¼ Cup of Mint, Fresh and Roughly Chopped
- 8 Ounces of Noodles, Rice Variety
- 1 Pomegranate, Fresh and Arils Only
- Ingredients for Your Chickpeas:

- 2, 15 Ounce Cans of Chickpeas, Drained and Rinsed

- 3 Tbsp. of Olive Oil, Extra Virgin Variety

- 1 tsp. of Cinnamon, Ground Variety

- 1 tsp. of Brown Sugar, Light and Packed

- Dash of Salt and Pepper, For Taste

Directions:

1. First place a large sized pot over medium heat. Add in your oil and once your oil is hot enough add in your minced garlic, ginger, pepper and green onions. Stir thoroughly to combine and cook for at least 3 to 5 minutes or until soft to the touch.

2. Add in your homemade broth along with your pumpkin. Bring your soup to a boil before reducing the heat to low. Allow to simmer for the next 15 to 20 minutes or until your pumpkin is tender to the touch.

3. Add at least ¾ of your soup into a blender. Blend on the highest setting until smooth in consistency. Return this back to your soup and stir thoroughly to combine.

4. Add in your peanut butter, favorite kind of soy sauce, fresh fish sauce and milk. Stir thoroughly to combine and add in your broccoli. Cook until tender to the touch. This should take at least 8 to 10 minutes.

5. During this time cook your rice noodles according to the directions on the package.

6. Remove your soup from heat and add in your egg noodles.

7. Make your chickpeas during this time. To do this first preheat your oven to 425 degrees.

8. Dry your chickpeas with a few paper towels and add to a baking sheet. Toss with your oil, ground cinnamon, light brown sugar and dash of salt and pepper. Place into your oven to roast for the next 20 minutes. After this time stir your chickpeas and roast for another 20 minutes or until brown and crunchy.

9. Remove and add to your soup. Stir to combine and serve your soup while piping hot.

Roasted Garlic and Pumpkin Hummus

Looking for a tasty dish to serve up during your next party event? Then this is the perfect dish for you to make. Serve this dip with fresh pita chips or your favorite kind of bread for the tastiest results.

Makes: 6 Servings

Total Prep Time: 30 Minutes

Ingredients:

- 1 to 2 Cloves of Garlic, Roasted

- 2 Tbsp. of Olive Oil, Extra Virgin Variety

- 2 Tbsp. of Water, Warm

- 1, 4 Ounce Can of Chickpeas, Drained and Rinsed

- 2/3 Cup of Pumpkin, Canned Variety

- 1 Tbsp. of Honey, Raw

- ½ tsp. of Rosemary, Fresh and Minced

- Dash of Salt, For Taste

Directions:

1. The first thing that you will want to do is roast your garlic. To do this place your peeled cloves into a small sized saucepan with some oil. Cook over low to medium heat for the next 15 to 20 minutes. Transfer to a blender.

2. Add all of your remaining ingredients except for your rosemary into your blender. Blend on the highest setting until smooth in consistency. Feel free to add more oil if you need to.

3. Transfer your mixture into a medium sized saucepan. Heat until piping hot and serve while still warm. Enjoy.

Tasty Pumpkin Brie Quesadillas

While traditional quesadillas are delicious themselves, there is no other quesadilla recipe that can quite compare to this one. For the tastiest results feel free to pack this quesadilla recipe with your favorite ingredients.

Makes: 4 Servings

Total Prep Time: 12 Minutes

Ingredients:

- 1 ¾ Cup of Pumpkin, Canned and Pure

- 1 tsp. of Chili, Powdered Variety

- 1 tsp. of Sage, Fresh and Minced

- ¼ tsp. of Cayenne Pepper, For Taste

- Some Cooking Spray

- 8 Tortillas, Floured Variety and Small in Size

- 5 Ounces of Brie Cheese, Sliced Thinly

Directions:

1. Use a small sized bowl and add in your pumpkin, powdered chili, sage and dash of cayenne pepper.

2. Heat up a large sized griddle placed over medium heat. Grease with some cooking spray and place your tortillas on top. Top each of your tortillas with some of your pumpkin mixture and some of your cheese. Top off with your tortillas.

3. Cook for at least 4 to 6 minutes or until your tortillas are gold in color and your cheese is fully melted.

4. Remove and cut in half prior to serving.

Hearty Pumpkin, Spinach and Walnut Smothered Spaghetti

Here is a delicious spaghetti dish that I know you won't be able to resist. Packed full of healthy ingredients such as pumpkin and spinach, this is yet another dish you never have to feel guilty about enjoying.

Makes: 2 Servings

Total Prep Time: 35 Minute

Ingredients:

- ¾ Cup of Spaghetti, Gluten Free Variety

- 3 Tbsp. of Olive Oil, Extra Virgin Variety

- 2 Cups of Butternut Squash, Cut into Small Sized Cubes

- ½ Cup of Spinach, Fresh and Roughly Chopped

- 1 tsp. of Chili Flakes, Crushed

- ½ of a Lemon, Fresh, Zest and Juice Only

- Dash of Salt and Pepper, For Taste

- 2 Tbsp. of Walnuts, Finely Chopped and Optional

Directions:

1. The first thing that you will want to do is coat your pumpkin in at least one spoonful of your oil and a dash of salt. Place onto a large sized baking tray and place into your oven to bake at 435 degrees. For at least 40 to 50 minutes or until soft to the touch.

2. Next heat up some oil in a large sized skillet placed over medium heat. Once your oil is hot enough add in your garlic and cook for at least a minute or two, making sure to stir frequently. Add in a dash of crushed red pepper flakes.

3. While your pumpkin is roasting cook your pasta according to the directions on the package.

4. Remove your pumpkin from your oven and mash at least half in a blender until smooth in consistency.

5. Add your cooked pasta and spinach to your skillet along with your pumpkin. Stir thoroughly to combine. Season with a dash of salt and pepper. Add some fresh lemon juice and serve immediately. Garnish with your walnuts and fresh lemon zest.

Pumpkin Grilled Cheese

Last but not least we have this delicious grilled cheese sandwich that children and adults alike are going to fall in love with. This is a great sandwich recipe to make if you are tight on time or want something quick and easy to prepare.

Makes: 4 Servings

Total Prep Time: 1 Hour and 30 Minutes

Ingredients:

- 1, 14 Pound Pumpkin, cut into Small Sized Pieces and Roasted
- 8 to 12 Ounces of Cheese, Gruyere Variety and Freshly Grated
- 8 Slices of Bread, Sourdough Variety
- 4 Tbsp. of Butter, Unsalted Variety and Soft
- 1 Tbsp. of Brown Sugar, Light and Packed
- 1 tsp. of Salt, For Taste
- 1 tsp. of Chili, Powdered Variety
- 1 tsp. of Paprika

Directions:

1. The first thing that you will want to do is split your pumpkin in half. Scrape out the seeds and insides. Place onto a large sized baking sheet with the cut side down and place into your oven to bake for the next 30 minutes. After this time flip your pumpkin so the cut side is facing up and roast for another 30 minutes.

2. Remove from your oven and allow your pumpkin to cool slightly. Scoop out the flesh of your pumpkin and mash roughly with a fork until smooth in consistency.

3. Add your brown sugar, dash of salt, powdered chili and dash of paprika into a small sized bowl. Stir to thoroughly combine.

4. Butter at least one side of your bread. Place the buttered side onto a large sized skillet and place over medium heat. Scoop at least half a cup of your pumpkin onto your bread. Sprinkle your spice mixture and freshly grate cheese over the top and top off with your bread, butter side up.

5. Cook your sandwich for at least 5 minutes before flipping. Continue to cook for another 5 minutes or until your bread is brown in color and your cheese is fully cooked. Remove and serve immediately.

Conclusion

Well, there you have it!

Hopefully by the end of this book you have learned how to prepare pumpkin the way that it was meant to be prepared. I hope that by the end of this book you have found the over 25 delicious pumpkin recipes to be perfect especially for this time of the year and have also found that they are also incredibly easy to prepare.

So, what is the next step for you?

The next step for you to take is to begin making all of the pumpkin recipes you have found in this book. Remember, during the fall season is when making these dishes is as ideal and feel free to add in your favorite ingredients into these dishes to make them truly unique.

Good luck!

About the Author

Hello my name is Ted Alling,

For as long as I can remember, I have always loved cooking and spending time in the kitchen. I honestly thought that my mother had dedicated her life to cooking, but later on in life, I came to understand that she was just a great stay at home mom of 4. Although I was a boy, I was always the only one interested in helping my mom make pancakes, fried eggs, and bratwurst. She proceeded to teach me how to make pasta, to cook chicken, stuff cabbages, and even how to make a pretty good risotto.

Life in Germany was wonderful as a kid, but my parents decided to move to the United States, or more specifically to the state of Illinois, in 1990. When I moved out to go to college in Georgia, not only was I able to make some delicious dishes, but I was a very popular roommate to have—I was one of the very rare ones who could prepare something other than mac & cheese from the box. The other students from the dorm really dug my special fried rice. Until this day, I won't give out the secret ingredient that makes it unique…

I graduated from college with honors and an accounting degree in 1995, and soon after started working in a firm in downtown Atlanta. All I could think about all day was what I would make for my girlfriend for dinner. She obviously did not mind that I had taken over the kitchen early on in our relationship. She is a nurse, and often has to work long hours and comes home exhausted and hungry.

However, food had become much more than a hobby or necessity for me…it was actually closer to an obsession, but I prefer to use the term passion. I was spending most of my weekends visiting fresh local markets and discovering new produce and herbs. After working as an accountant for 5 years, I realized that life was far too short to continue missing out on my true calling: cooking.

I applied as a part time cook at a local diner about 10 minutes from home, and the rest, as they say, is history. Three years later I was opening my own restaurant with my wife as my main partner. All my ex-fellow accountants now come in to eat at lunch time. We have been serving our clientele my famous fried rice, and many more dishes that I will be glad to share with you over the future weeks.

What makes me a good chef? My passion for food, and the fresher the ingredients, the better. I love to experiment with flavors and I dare you to do the same. Sure, we all have our favorites, but don't settle in your ways. Be creative. Play with the colors, the herbs, the spices, the types of meat, fruits, and vegetables. Grow your own garden and talk to your butcher about trying different cuts of meat that he has to offer on a weekly basis.

Now, I have to go back to the kitchen, but next time you feel like preparing a mouthwatering dish, please stop by, and I will make sure to share "most" of my secrets.

Author's Afterthoughts

Thanks ever so much to each of my cherished readers for investing the time to read this book!

I know you could have picked from many other books but you chose this one. So a big thanks for downloading this book and reading all the way to the end.

If you enjoyed this book or received value from it, I'd like to ask you for a favor. Please take a few minutes to post an honest and heartfelt review on Amazon.com. Your support does make a difference and helps to benefit other people.

Thanks!

Ted Alling

Made in the USA
San Bernardino, CA
20 November 2016